HO HO HO, HA HA HA

North Pole

Holly-arious Christmas
Knock-Knock Jokes

By KATY HALL and LISA EISENBERG
Pictures by STEVE BJÖRKMAN

HARPER FESTIVAL
An Imprint of HarperCollins Publishers

Knock, knock!
    Who's there?
Waddle!
    Waddle who?
Waddle we do to find Santa?

Knock, knock!
  Who's there?
Snow!
  Snow who?

Knock, knock!
  Who's there?
Icy!
  Icy who?
Icy which way to go now!

Knock, knock!
Who's there?
Stopwatch!

Stopwatch who?

Knock, knock!
Who's there?
Gift!
Gift who?
Gift to me, and I'll help
you wrap it over again.

Knock, knock!
Who's there?
Luke!
Luke who?
Luke that way
for Santa!

Knock, knock!
    Who's there?
Ribbon!
    Ribbon who?

Knock, knock!
Who's there?
Hoof!
Hoof who?
Hoof you seen
Santa Claus
anywhere around here?

Knock, knock!
Who's there?
Dasher!
Dasher who?
Dasher is a pretty
reindeer!

Knock, knock!
Who's there?
Wendy!
Wendy who?
Wendy sleigh is ready,
let me know.

Knock, knock!
Who's there?
Polar!
Polar who?
Polar part of the sleigh,
and I'll pull mine!

Knock, knock!
  Who's there?
Yule!
    Yule who?

Knock, knock!
    Who's there?
Wreath!
    Wreath who?
Wreath think you'll
like our letter, Santa.

Knock, knock.
    Who's there?
Winter!
    Winter who?
Winter we leave?

Knock, knock!
Who's there?

Murray!
Murray who?